Natalie du Toit

**A biography
by Alison Hawes**

Contents

Introduction	2
Becoming a champion	4
Overcoming tragedy	10
Back on top	16
Looking ahead	22
Glossary	24

GW01551382

Introduction

As a young child, Natalie du Toit was a very good swimmer. By the time she was fourteen years old she was swimming for her country. Her dream was to swim for her country at the **Olympic Games.**

Her dream was nearly shattered when one day, on her way to school, Natalie was hit by a car. She lost her left leg in the accident and her whole life changed.

Natalie started swimming when she was six.

People thought that Natalie would give up on her dream of swimming in the Olympics. They thought that no one with only one leg could be a champion swimmer. Natalie could have given up, but she did not. Being **disabled** was not going to get in the way of her dreams! This is her amazing story.

Natalie did not give up her dream of becoming a champion swimmer.

Becoming a champion

Learning to swim

SOUTH AFRICA

Natalie du Toit was born in Cape Town in South Africa on January 29th 1984. She still lives there today with her parents and her brother.

When she was very little, Natalie had **asthma.** Her parents thought it would help Natalie's asthma if she went swimming, but when Natalie first got in the pool she was scared of the water. She would hold on to the side of the pool and get out again as quickly as she could!

If Natalie's family went to the beach, Natalie wouldn't go into the sea. She hated being in the water, and refused to swim.

Then one day, when Natalie was six, she jumped in the pool and just started swimming. Everyone was amazed. After that it was difficult to get her out of the water!

Taking off!

Natalie went swimming as often as she could. She practised very hard, and became an excellent swimmer. As she got older, she started to compete in swimming races, and at the age of ten she began breaking **records** set by other swimmers. Four years later, Natalie won the South African Swimming Championships.

After that, Natalie was picked to swim with the South African team in the 1998 **Commonwealth Games.** She flew with the team to Malaysia where she swam in the 200-metre **butterfly** race. She was just fourteen years old.

Butterfly is the most demanding swimming stroke. It requires high levels of fitness and upper-body strength.

The next year Natalie swam in many more races, and won two silver medals at the All Africa Games. The games were held in Natalie's home country of South Africa.

Natalie was one of the 6 000 sportspeople that took part in the 1999 All Africa Games. The opening ceremony took place in the Johannesburg Stadium.

Early morning training sessions helped to turn Natalie into a champion swimmer.

Natalie hoped she would be picked for the Olympic Team in the year 2000, but her swimming times were not quite fast enough. Natalie decided she must train harder. That meant getting up for more early-morning swimming lessons, followed by a full day of lessons at school!

Then something terrible happened …

Overcoming tragedy

A terrible accident

It was February 26th 2001, four weeks after Natalie's seventeenth birthday. Natalie had just been for a swimming lesson and she was riding her scooter to school. Suddenly, she was hit by a car. The car ran over her left leg, crushing it badly.

Natalie was rushed to hospital. For seven days, the doctors tried to save her left leg, but it was so badly damaged that in the end they had to **amputate** it at the knee.

Natalie's life was turned upside down. It looked like her days as a champion swimmer were over.

Natalie at home recovering after her operation

Fighting back

No one knew whether Natalie would swim again. No one except Natalie, that is. She had two choices – she could give up on her dreams and accept that she would never swim properly again, or she could fight back and overcome her **disability.**

Swimming was such a big part of Natalie's life that she missed it terribly. She decided while she was in hospital that she had to fight back, and she made up her mind to start swimming again as soon as she could.

In fact, Natalie was back in the pool only three months after her accident, before she could even walk!

osing her leg was not going to stop
Natalie from swimming.

When she first went to the pool after the accident, Natalie wasn't sure what she would be able to do. She was scared that she wouldn't be able to do anything at all. She hoped that she would at least be able to float in the pool. Natalie surprised everyone, including herself, by staying in the pool for two hours on her first visit and actually doing some swimming!

At first, learning to swim again was difficult and painful for Natalie. When she wasn't swimming, Natalie wore a **prosthetic** leg, but she took this leg off when she went swimming.

Swimming with one leg was very difficult. First, Natalie had to learn how to rebalance herself in the water. Then she had to learn to use her arms and upper body more than her leg, to help her swim faster.

Natalie worked very hard and spent many hours trying to learn how to swim with just one leg. She was determined to become fast enough to compete again. Helped by her coach, Natalie learned how to swim almost as fast as she could before her accident! Amazingly, just one year after losing her leg, Natalie was picked to swim for South Africa in the Commonwealth Games again.

Natalie swims without her prosthetic leg.

Back on top

Going for gold

The 2002 Commonwealth Games were held in Manchester in England. This was Natalie's first big competition since her accident. She was nervous that she might not swim fast enough, but she wanted to show the world that she would not let her disability stop her from trying to win.

Natalie swam in three races. The 50-metre and the 100-metre **freestyle** events were for disabled swimmers, like Natalie. Not only did Natalie win the gold medal in both these events, she also broke both world records!

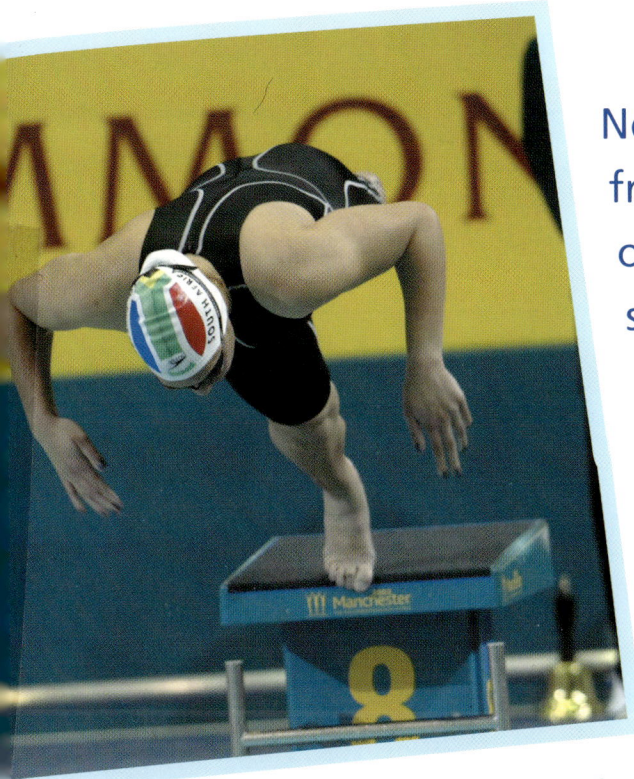

Natalie won two gold medals at the 2002 Commonwealth Games.

Natalie's third race was the 800-metre freestyle. It was different from her other races, as it was for **able-bodied** swimmers. Natalie was the only disabled swimmer in the race. She swam so well that she got to the final. She didn't win a medal in the final, but she didn't mind – she had beaten so many able-bodied swimmers to get there! She swam 800 metres in only 9 minutes and 13.57 seconds. It was an amazing achievement.

Fantastic first

Natalie was the first person to compete in both able-bodied and disabled races at the same Games. She showed the world that she could overcome her disability and swim like a champion. Swimming made her forget that she was disabled at all.

Natalie said: "The water is a gift that gives me back my leg. I remember the thrill of the first time that I swam after the operation — it felt like my leg was there. It still does."

People were so impressed at Natalie's achievement that they gave her an award. She was named the outstanding athlete of the Commonwealth Games. She even met the Queen!

Natalie won the award for the outstanding athlete of the Commonwealth Games.

More medals

After the Games, Natalie went back to school in South Africa. She continued to train for three hours every day, and to compete in races. Sometimes she swam in races for disabled people, and sometimes she swam in races for able-bodied people.

Natalie was named South African Sportswoman of the Year in 2002.

In July 2003, Natalie beat her own world record for the 100-metre freestyle race. In October, she won a gold medal at the All Africa Games in the 800-metre freestyle race, swimming against able-bodied swimmers.

Natalie helped raise money that year for a special school in Cape Town. She did this by swimming eight miles from Cape Town to Robben Island and back. Natalie also started encouraging other disabled people to achieve their dreams. She started trying to bring able-bodied and disabled people together, to help them understand each other better.

Natalie makes public appearances to improve understanding between able-bodied and disabled people.

Looking ahead

Natalie once said: "I just want to be me before the accident going for goals, going for dreams." And this is what she is doing.

One of her goals is to compete in swimming events until she is thirty years old. Another goal is to go to university. And of course, Natalie still has her dream of swimming in the Olympics. "I know it will be tough, but I'm determined to achieve it," she said. "I believe if you put your mind to it anything is possible."

Natalie and her mother

Glossary

able-bodied	not **disabled**
amputate	to cut off
asthma	an illness that can make it difficult to breathe
butterfly	a stroke in swimming
Commonwealth Games	a big sports event held every four years for athletes from 57 countries around the world
disability	something about your body that makes it difficult for you to easily do some everyday activities
disabled	to have a **disability**
freestyle	a swimming race in which any stroke can be used
Olympic Games	a big sports event held every four years between teams from all over the world
prosthetic	using a man-made part to replace a missing part of the body
record	the best so far, such as the fastest time in which a race is run